WHO'S THE KING?
AN AFFIRMATION STORY

**WRITTEN BY JAMAL
AND CAIRO KELLY**

**ILLUSTRATED BY
MICHON PITTMAN**

WHO'S THE KING is a story about a young boy named Cairo, who after watching his father create goals and affirmations for the upcoming year, decides he wants an affirmation of his own. Cairo becomes so excited about his new affirmation and how it makes him feel, he recites it morning, noon, and night. His feeling of self worth and pride is taken to new heights. Cairo recognizes himself as a young king and teaches and inspires others to do the same.

FOREWORD

who's the king
is supreme
fabulous
fantastic
and amazing

— CAIRO

It was the start of the New Year. It was time to think about last year's accomplishments and create new goals. Cairo walked into his father's office.

"Happy New Year," said his father. "Happy
New Year!" said Cairo.

"What are you doing?" asked Cairo.

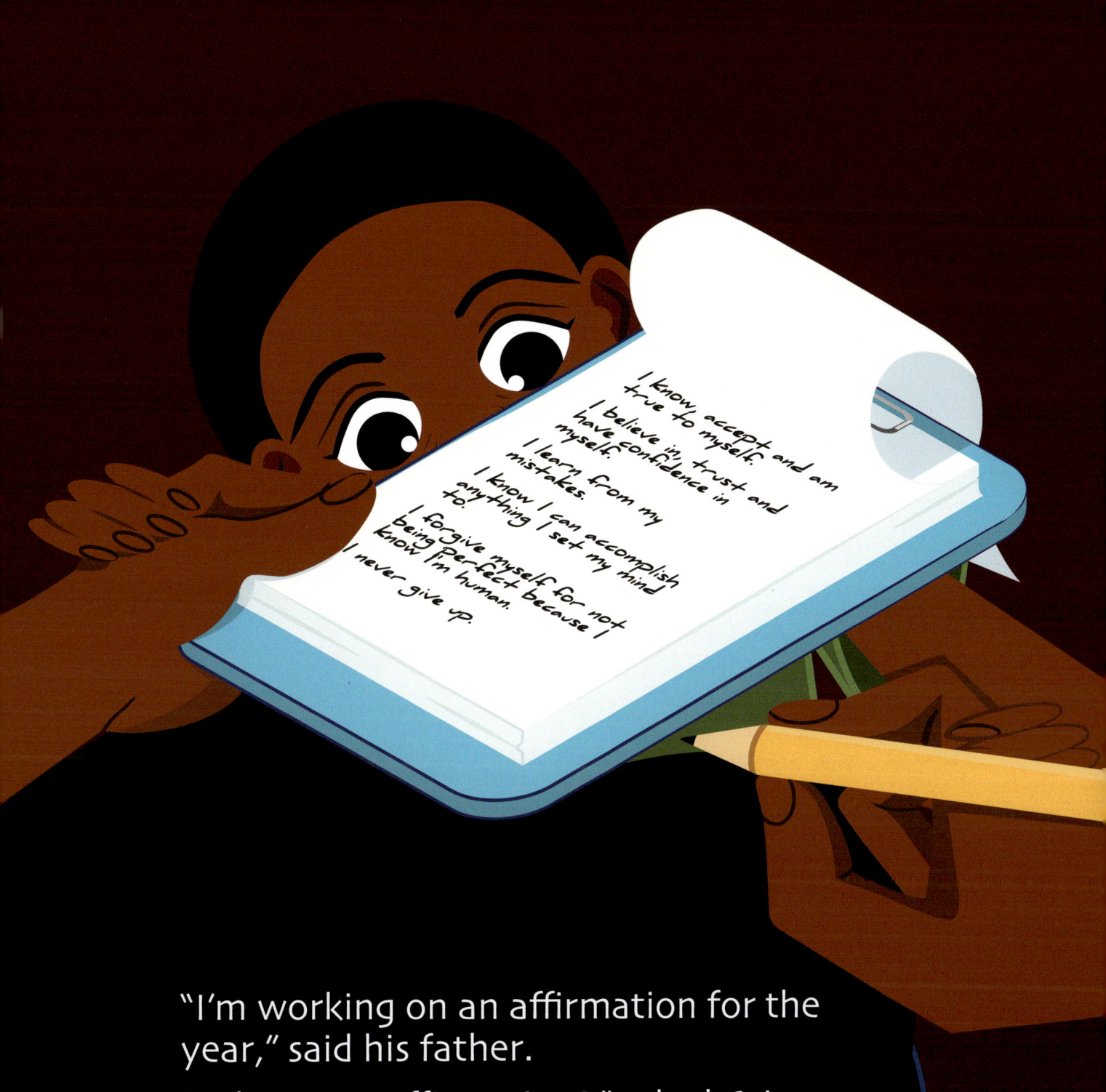

"I'm working on an affirmation for the year," said his father.

"What is an affirmation?" asked Cairo.

"An affirmation is a statement that is said to make us feel good about ourselves. It can be a simple statement or paragraph."

ENTHUSIASM!

"When you state your affirmation, say it with enthusiasm!" said his father.

"Do you mean like this?!" shouted Cairo loudly.

"Yes son, yes! Just like that!" laughed Cairo's father.

"Dad, do you have an affirmation?" asked

"Absolutely," replied his father.

"What is it?" asked Cairo.

"I believe in myself and my abilities. I am destined for greatness!"

"Cool!" said Cairo.

"Can you help me with my affirmation?"
"Of course," said his father.

"First, I want you to understand you are a king and equal to any and everyone in this world."

"I am a king?" asked Cairo.

"Yes, you are," his father replied.

"I am a king", said Cairo.
"Say it again," said his father.
"I am a king!" Cairo said boldly.
"Good job!"

"When I say, 'who's the king, you say,
'King Cairo!'"

"Who's the king?"

"King Cairo!!!"

"Who's the king?"

"King Cairo!!!"

"Who's the king?"

"King Cairo!!!"

"How did that make you feel?" asked his father.

"It felt great!" replied Cairo.

Cairo walked around the house reciting his affirmation, smiling throughout the day!

Cairo recited his affirmation in the morning, afternoon, and evening.

He recited his affirmation before a game, a test, and anytime he needed a boost of positivity and confidence.

One day at school, Cairo saw his cousin Kendall. He was sitting on the steps and appeared to be sad.

"What's wrong?" asked Cairo.

"I'm having a rough day," said Kendall.

"Kendall, do you know what an affirmation is?"

"No, what's an affirmation?" asked Kendall.

Cairo sat down beside his cousin and began to teach him how affirmations work.

Each one, teach one!!!

Affirmation examples

❖ "I believe in myself and my abilities!"

❖ "I am awesome!"

❖ "I am destined for greatness!"

❖ "I am intelligent!"

❖ "I control how I feel!"

❖ "I am powerful!"

❖ "I am beautiful!"

❖ "I am in charge of my choices!"

❖ "I am determined!"

❖ "I will communicate my true feelings!"

❖ "I will rely on those I trust!"

❖ "I am worthy of respect so I give it to others!"

❖ "I am important!"

CREATE YOUR OWN AFFIRMATIONS

_____

_____

_____

_____

_____

_____

_____

_____

_____

_____

_____

_____

DON'T FORGET TO TEACH YOUR FRIENDS ABOUT AFFIRMATIONS!
THANK YOU!

About the Authors

Jamal Kelly was born and raised in Bridgeport, Connecticut. He is a graduate of Virginia Union University and currently works in the behavioral and mental health field at All Family Matters, Inc. He is a member of Omega Psi Phi Fraternity, Incorporated where he serves as Chairman of the Omega Stars Youth Academy. He volunteers as a fill in father at the annual Date with Dad dance sponsored by Camp Diva, a nonprofit organization in Richmond, Va. His hobbies are reading, music, and sports. His motto is "Nothing changes if nothing changes".

About the Illustrator

Michon Pittman is an illustrator from Richmond, Virginia. She has a bachelor of Fine Arts in Communication Arts from Virginia Commonwealth University. She enjoys JazzHop, the color red, tea and drawing while reading. She is very likely doing the latter right now.